# THE
# KADDISH
# MINYAN

## THE IMPACT ON TEN LIVES

*A series of reflections on
saying Kaddish for a loved one*

## EDITED WITH AN INTRODUCTION BY
## RABBI HERBERT A. YOSKOWITZ

EAKIN PRESS ⱱ𝕡 Austin, Texas

FIRST EDITION
Copyright © 2001
By Rabbi Herbert A. Yoskowitz
Published in the United States of America
By Eakin Press
A Division of Sunbelt Media, Inc.
P.O. Drawer 90159 ☜ Austin, Texas 78709-0159
email: eakinpub@sig.net
💻 website: www.eakinpress.com 💻
ALL RIGHTS RESERVED.
1   2   3   4   5   6   7   8   9
**1-57168-595-2 PB**
**1-57168-596-0 HB**

For CIP information, please access:
www.loc.gov

The first excerpt on page 50 ("Tradition") is reprinted with permission from the Central Conference of American Rabbis. The excerpt on pages 50-51 ("The Kaddish") is reprinted with permission from The Prayer Book Press of Media Judaica, Inc. The last excerpt on p. 51 ("Personal Meditation") and excerpts on pages xv-xvii are reprinted with permission of The Rabbinical Assembly.

# THE
# KADDISH
# MINYAN

Dedication

To my family, especially to my wife, Rachel, who faithfully said Kaddish for her mother during the year of mourning. She served as a model for our family on the way to respect a parent when there would be no "thank you" forthcoming.

# Contents

# Personal Page

## Name of Deceased

English Name: _____

Hebrew Name: _____

## Date of Death (*Yahrzeit*)

English Date: _____

Hebrew Date: _____

## Conclusion of Shloshim (first thirty days of mourning)

English Date: _____

Hebrew Date: _____

## Conclusion of eleven months of Kaddish

English Date: _____

Hebrew Date: _____

## Dates of Yizkor

English Dates: _____

Hebrew Dates: _____

# Personal Page

## Name of Deceased

English Name: _____

Hebrew Name: _____

## Date of Death (*Yahrzeit*)

English Date: _____

Hebrew Date: _____

## Conclusion of Shloshim (first thirty days of mourning)

English Date: _____

Hebrew Date: _____

## Conclusion of eleven months of Kaddish

English Date: _____

Hebrew Date: _____

## Dates of Yizkor

English Dates: _____

Hebrew Dates: _____

# Personal Page

## Name of Deceased

English Name: _____

Hebrew Name: _____

## Date of Death (*Yahrzeit*)

English Date: _____

Hebrew Date: _____

## Conclusion of Shloshim (first thirty days of mourning)

English Date: _____

Hebrew Date: _____

## Conclusion of eleven months of Kaddish

English Date: _____

Hebrew Date: _____

## Dates of Yizkor

English Dates: _____

Hebrew Dates: _____

# Personal Page

## Name of Deceased

English Name: _____

Hebrew Name: _____

## Date of Death (*Yahrzeit*)

English Date: _____

Hebrew Date: _____

## Conclusion of Shloshim (first thirty days of mourning)

English Date: _____

Hebrew Date: _____

## Conclusion of eleven months of Kaddish

English Date: _____

Hebrew Date: _____

## Dates of Yizkor

English Dates: _____

Hebrew Dates: _____

# Foreword to *The Kaddish Minyan*

The Jewish spirit heals through community and tradition. It is through these two interacting spheres of text and context, of Torah and fellow travelers, that we reach for strength, support, meaning, and guidance. Sometimes we may achieve profound inspiration or uplifting transcendence—and sometimes we simply manage to make it from Monday to Tuesday, in one reasonably intact piece.

This wonderful publication reflects the encounter of Jews wounded by the death of a dear one with the depth and breadth of remarkable structures: the ancient words of the *Kaddish*, and the contemporary *Kaddish minyan*. The open, honest voices of these mourners weave an extended family, a "meta-minyan," of empathic, attentive Jews, and simultaneously invite us to recount and listen to our own inner narratives of loss, survival, and growth. Let the information and insight on these pages illumine your own path through grief and inform your efforts to be present with, and supportive of, others in their time of need.

Just as the bereavement extends way beyond the initial shiva week, the shloshim month, and the first year of loss, so the spiritual resources of words and fellowship are ever there for struggle and renewal. *The Kaddish Minyan* models how the memory of a loved one might be restated, rekindled, and revisited; and, as time goes by, how the healing narrative can grow to include anecdotes about that very remembering, about our rebuilding and reaffirming.

This, then, is not only about the journey towards affirming the Sacred in the midst of loss, pain, and despair; it is an echo, a refraction of that very Wholeness and Eternity, much like the Kaddish prayer itself. It is a chorus of searching, soulful Jews, wanting to heal but also willing to help heal others, most of whom they will never know.

RABBI SIMKHA Y. WEINTRAUB, CSW
Rabbinic Director,
National Center for Jewish Healing

# Acknowledgments

On a balmy, November 1999 evening at Adat Shalom Synagogue in Farmington Hills, Michigan, I was blessed to be a part of the most memorable adult education program of my thirty-year rabbinic career.

Never before had I experienced emotion such as was expressed during that evening when congregants came forward to discuss what Kaddish means to them. It was a unique moment in time when all of us were at one, enveloped in thoughts of what Kaddish and the Kaddish Minyan can do for Jews in the throes of dealing with loss. It was this experience and the dialogue afterwards that led to this book.

To all those who were present at the birth of this publication on that evening at Adult Jewish Education, I am indebted.

To my dedicated clergy colleagues at Adat Shalom, whose words and support aided this publication, I am appreciative.

To the congregation's leadership who encouraged and reviewed this manuscript as it evolved—Dr. Michael Gellis, Terran Leemis, Beverly Liss, and Larry Wolfe—I am thankful. I treasure the time we spent discussing this manuscript in my office.

To the loyal readers of this manuscript, including Rabbi Samuel Stahl, Reverend David Blewett, Bill Liberson and David Techner, I am grateful. They critiqued my work and expanded the possibilities of this book to serve both Jews and non-Jews. I am in your debt.

To my secretary, Charlotte Fiszbein, who was very helpful in preparing drafts of this publication, I am indebted.

To Ed Eakin and Virginia Messer, publisher and associate publisher at Eakin Press, and to Melissa Locke Roberts, editor, I express much appreciation.

To Rabbi Simkha Weintraub of The National Center for Jewish Healing, whose dialogues with me about the Kaddish Minyan increased my enthusiasm to move it towards publication even as his comments made the book's message more poignant, I am relishing the memories of our interesting conversations.

To all those who contributed their reflections on saying Kaddish for a loved one, I am filled with admiration. Their essays are the core content of this book. These wonderful people were willing to share of themselves even in the midst of their grief. They have my deep respect and gratitude.

—HERBERT A. YOSKOWITZ
Farmington Hills, Michigan
June 2001

# Mourner's Kaddish

*Mourners and those observing Yahrzeit:*

יִתְגַּדַּל וְיִתְקַדַּשׁ שְׁמֵהּ רַבָּא. בְּעָלְמָא דִּי בְרָא כִרְעוּתֵהּ, וְיַמְלִיךְ
מַלְכוּתֵהּ בְּחַיֵּיכוֹן וּבְיוֹמֵיכוֹן וּבְחַיֵּי דְכָל בֵּית יִשְׂרָאֵל. בַּעֲגָלָא וּבִזְמַן
קָרִיב וְאִמְרוּ אָמֵן׃

*Congregation and mourner:*

יְהֵא שְׁמֵהּ רַבָּא מְבָרַךְ לְעָלַם וּלְעָלְמֵי עָלְמַיָּא׃

*Mourner:*

יִתְבָּרַךְ וְיִשְׁתַּבַּח, וְיִתְפָּאַר וְיִתְרוֹמַם וְיִתְנַשֵּׂא וְיִתְהַדָּר וְיִתְעַלֶּה
וְיִתְהַלָּל שְׁמֵהּ דְּקֻדְשָׁא בְּרִיךְ הוּא לְעֵלָּא מִן כָּל בִּרְכָתָא וְשִׁירָתָא,
תֻּשְׁבְּחָתָא וְנֶחֱמָתָא, דַּאֲמִירָן בְּעָלְמָא, וְאִמְרוּ אָמֵן׃
יְהֵא שְׁלָמָא רַבָּא מִן שְׁמַיָּא וְחַיִּים עָלֵינוּ וְעַל כָּל יִשְׂרָאֵל, וְאִמְרוּ
אָמֵן׃
עֹשֶׂה שָׁלוֹם בִּמְרוֹמָיו הוּא יַעֲשֶׂה שָׁלוֹם עָלֵינוּ וְעַל כָּל יִשְׂרָאֵל,
וְאִמְרוּ אָמֵן׃

Yitgadal v'yitkadash sh'mei raba b'alma di v'ra khir'utei,
v'yamlikh malkhutei b'hayeikhon u-v'yomeikhon u-v'hayei
d'khol beit yisrael, ba-agala u-vi-z'man kariv v'imru amen.

Y'hei sh'mei raba m'vorakh l'alam u-l'almei almaya.

Yitbarakh v'yishtabah v'yitpa'ar v'yitromam v'yitnasei,
v'yit-hadar v'yit'aleh v'yit-halal sh'mei d'kudsha, b'rikh
hu l'ela (l'ela mi-kol) min kol birkhata v'shirata, tushb'hata
v'nehemata da-amiran b'alma, v'imru amen.

Y'hei shlama raba min sh'maya v'hayim aleinu v'al kol yisrael, v'imru amen.

Oseh shalom bi-m'romav, hu ya'aseh shalom aleinu v'al kol
yisrael, v'imru amen.

_____

Hallowed and enhanced may He be throughout the world
of His own creation. May He cause His sovereignty soon to
be accepted, during our life and the life of all Israel. And let
us say: Amen.

May He be praised throughout all time.

Glorified and celebrated, lauded and worshipped, acclaimed
and honored, extolled and exalted may the Holy One be,
praised beyond all song and psalm, beyond all tributes
which mortals can utter. And let us say: Amen.

Let there be abundant peace from Heaven, with life's
goodness for us and for all the people Israel.
And let us say: Amen.

He who brings peace to His universe will bring peace to us
and to all the people Israel. And let us say: Amen.

---

Our Creator, the King of kings, delights in life. Because of His
love for us, and because we are so few, each of us is important in His kingdom. Though we are flesh and blood, we are
irreplaceable. When one of the House of Israel dies, there is
a loss of glory in His kingdom and His grandeur is diminished. Therefore, members of the House of Israel, all of you
who mourn and all of you who remember on this day, let us
fix our hearts on our Father in Heaven, our King and our
Redeemer, and let us pray for ourselves, and for Him too, that
He and His sovereignty be hallowed and enhanced, glorified
and celebrated.

---

(Reprinted from *Siddur Sim Shalom*,
edited by Rabbi Jules Harlow,
pages 524-525. Copyright by
The Rabbinical Assembly, 1985.
Reprinted by permission
of The Rabbinical Assembly.)

*"The Jewish way of mourning has turned an absence into a presence."*

—from Leon Wieseltier's *The Kaddish*

# I.

## INTRODUCTION

By Rabbi Herbert A. Yoskowitz

## Why Kaddish? The Impetus for This Book

The Kaddish evokes a stronger emotional response in Jews than any other prayer in our liturgy. It is recited evening, morning, and afternoon by Jews all over the world; by the richest and the humblest; by the young and the old; by the sophisticated and the simple. Some Jews who otherwise do not adhere to other Jewish traditions faithfully say the Kaddish for eleven months after a parent dies and subsequently during each year on the parent's *yahrzeit*.

Yet, with all the recitation of the Kaddish, to most the Kaddish is shrouded in mystery. Many people in the congregation ask about the Kaddish: its origin, meaning and custom. In response to the many queries, we realized the need to formally present a series of programs on this meaningful prayer.

The programs were well received. In particular, one session had a profound impact on those who attended. At this session I introduced the subject and the panel of mourners, three still in their year of mourning and one who had just completed his eleven months of saying Kaddish. The four of them and I spoke. They were mourning the death of a child, of a parent, and of a spouse. Their words touched the souls of those in attendance.

1

In addition, funeral directors were invited to share taped messages on "The Impact of Kaddish," excerpts of which were shared after the panel of mourners spoke.

One member of the congregation who could not be present contributed her comments after the panel presentations. At a later time, two other congregants and a non-congregant who heard about our program contributed their comments about the impact of Kaddish on them. Colleagues of mine at Adat Shalom Synagogue added their perspectives on the Kaddish.

This book provides a brief introduction to the Kaddish and an appreciation of what the Kaddish can do for the mourner during the required period of saying Kaddish. Its uniqueness lies in the personal views of those who have experienced the phenomena of saying Kaddish. The power of life stories is that we see ourselves in others. When people cope with the ultimate boundary of this life—that is, death—we can be strengthened as we experience our own grief. We are not alone but are a part of a community that shares the universal experience of death. Our own fears are echoed in memories, hopes and prayers.

To read how others utilize Kaddish to help them during their grief is reassuring for our own journey. Their messages of the impact of Kaddish on the mourner are more powerful than anything a Rabbi, "the defender of the faith," can offer. When congregants write how Kaddish helps them, their words are more powerful than any that can be spoken from any pulpit by any powerful Rabbinic orator. When congregants attest to the power of Kaddish in their lives, a powerful message is broadcast. We are indebted to all those who shared their innermost feelings about their grief and about the impact of the Mourner's Kaddish on them.

It is my hope that the sharing of the experiences in this book will motivate mourners to say Kaddish to honor their deceased relatives and to support their journey of grief, remembrance and healing.

# A Brief Introduction
## to the Kaddish Prayer

While the Kaddish is thought to be a prayer for the dead, essentially it is an affirmation of life. Neither death nor the dead is mentioned.

Originally Kaddish was a response recited at the close of a Rabbinic lesson in the synagogue during the Talmudic Period (200 BCE–550 CE). A message of comfort and consolation would conclude the Rabbi's lesson. Kaddish extended that message by focusing on our messianic hope. This Kaddish is called the Rabbi's Kaddish.

In post-Talmudic time, saying the Kaddish was extended from the House of Study to the House of Prayer and ultimately to the cemetery. The Rabbis taught that Kaddish should be recited for eleven months for a deceased parent. For other deceased relatives, there was a thirty-day obligation to say Kaddish. Today, some choose to say Kaddish for eleven months in memory not just of parents but of other relatives, too.

Kaddish, an Aramaic word for "holy," praises God's name and must be said in public assembly, which is defined as a quorum of at least ten Jewish adults, a *minyan*. In addition to the Rabbi's Kaddish, other forms of Kaddish said during a religious service include the Full Kaddish recited at the end of a service, the Half Kaddish said at the conclusion of smaller prayer units, and the Mourner's Kaddish.

Kaddish is said subsequently by a mourner on the anniversary of the death (*yahrzeit*) of a loved one during all services on that day and on Yom Kippur, Succot, Pesach, and Shavuot when the Memorial Service (*Yizkor*) is recited. On the *yahrzeit*, it is customary for the mourner to receive an *aliyah*, an honor involving being called to the Torah and reciting Torah blessings expressing joyous sentiments. It is suggested that if the *yahrzeit* occurs on a non-Torah reading day, the person observing the *yahrzeit* should receive an *aliyah* (an opportunity to praise God while standing before the open Torah) in the synagogue on the Shabbat before the *yahrzeit*.

## Some of the Laws of Kaddish

Unsurpassed in Jewish law as a paean to God, the laws of Kaddish are of interest even to Jews who are otherwise indifferent to other aspects of Jewish observance.

The laws of Kaddish instruct us regarding basic questions, such as for whom do we say Kaddish, when may Kaddish be recited, for how long is Kaddish recited. There are more esoteric questions, such as how many times a day should a mourner say Kaddish, and must a son who bears a grudge against his deceased father say Kaddish for him, and under what circumstance may a person be paid to say kaddish? Here is a selection of laws that reflect our tradition's approach:

- Kaddish is required to be said for anyone for whom a mourner sits Shiva*: mother, father, son, daughter, husband, wife, brother and sister.

- Kaddish is recited for a parent for eleven months. For all other relatives for whom Kaddish is required, Kaddish is said for *Shloshim*, thirty days. People may elect to say Kaddish for other relatives and for friends, though it is customary not to say Kaddish for such people while parents are alive.

---

*Shiva is the obligatory seven-day mourning period that immediately follows burial.

4

- Only if a religious quorum (*minyan*) is present may one say Kaddish. If no *minyan* is present, the mourner should study a Jewish text in honor of the deceased but not recite the Kaddish. That study can be considered to be an act of sanctification.

- We are cautioned against saying the Mourner's Kaddish excessively. As one medieval Rabbi wrote, "I clamor against those who multiply the recitation of the Mourner's Kaddish any place and any time."

- A child who bears a grudge against a parent is required nonetheless to say Kaddish for that parent. To refrain from doing so reflects unfavorably not only on the memory of a parent but upon the child, too, and may hinder his/her ability to mourn—even to mourn the kind of parent she/he may not have had.

- Similarly, a child may ignore a parent's wish that Kaddish not be recited for the parent.

- If a deceased person has no relatives to recite Kaddish for him or for her, someone should be hired to say the Kaddish. The person saying the Kaddish should say these words before the prayer service begins, "All the Kaddishim I recite today are for the benefit of the soul of (name of the deceased)." Then he adds the words of Psalm 90:17: "May the favor of the Lord, our God, be upon us; let the work of our hands prosper, O prosper the work of our hands."

Consult your own Rabbinic authority with particular questions or concerns about saying Kaddish.

# The Kaddish and Immortality

The Kaddish does not mention death. Instead, the words focus on God's majesty, magnificence and sanctity. However, one Rabbinic story that is repeated many times in midrashic lore links the Kaddish to the souls of the deceased.

Rabbi Akiva walked near a graveyard and saw the soul (or spirit) of someone who had died. That soul is restless and disturbed. "Who are you," Rabbi Akiva asked, "and what have you done?"

The man said, "The man whom you are addressing is a dead man. Every day they send me out to chop wood."

"My son, what was your work in the world from which you came?"

"I was a tax collector, and I would favor the rich and kill the poor."

"Have your superiors told you nothing about how you might relieve your condition?"

"Please, sir, do not detain me, for you will irritate my tormentors. For such a man (as I), there can be no relief. Though I did hear them say something—but no, it is impossible. They said that if this poor man had a son, and his son were to stand before the congregation and recite (the prayer) 'Bless the Lord who is blessed!' and the congregation were to answer amen, and the son were also to say 'May the Great Name be blessed!' (a sentence from the Kaddish), they would release him from his punishment." (Wieseltier: *Kaddish*, page 41)

Thus, the Kaddish said by a child for a deceased parent is thought to improve the life of the immortal soul of the parent in the world-to-come. Now the lives of all the souls in the world-to-come are thought to be improved when Kaddish is recited for them collectively, such as when Kaddish is said for the Six Million or when Kaddish is recited for a specific deceased person. We say the Kaddish for loved ones who are in the world-to-come, and we bring their memories to mind in a heightened manner.

However, the world-to-come is described in Jewish sources, with its many and varied interpretations, as being tied to the hopes of the arrival of the Messianic period and of the resurrection of the dead.

The Messianic Era is part of the hope of what will happen after the physical life is ended. Healing the world—*Tikkun Olam*—is connected to the days of the Messiah. Healing the world, one of the strongest injunctions in Judaism, actually mirrors the ultimate Jewish hope for the afterlife.

The Kaddish gives us a hint of this connection. The Kaddish asks for the hastening of the day when the earth reflects Godliness. It describes a world in which God's perfection and the praises of God's name are so evident that God's world and the world on which human history unfolds become the same. It affirms the possibility of healing the world and calls for the peace of "God's high place" to be known here on earth. The goal of the Kaddish, in fact, is to bring together the two worlds of *Olam Hazeh*, our present existence, and *Olam Haba*, which in its ultimate form is the Messianic Era.

While resurrection of the dead in the distant future is usually interpreted as the bodily reconstitution of the deceased individual, it is depicted as the collective national revival of the entire Jewish people, too. Resurrection has come closest to acquiring the status of dogma in Jewish tradition. In the synagogue on Friday nights, it is sung in the concluding one of the thirteen articles of the *Yigdal* hymn, based on the creed of Maimonides and in the daily Amidah.

Maimonides' creed notwithstanding, there is no clearly iterated dogmatic position regarding what happens after we complete our physical life. There is a melding of many components in the eschatological visions across the ages and through to the present day.

Until that Messianic Era arrives, our Kaddish prayer links

us to the souls of our beloved whether we believe in the literal hope of the resurrection, which ties body and soul together as an inseparable spirit, or in the figurative interpretation that the immortal soul has a separate existence from the mortal body.

The Kaddish is clearly linked to our conviction that our souls are immortal. The souls of those who have died continue to influence our own souls; our spiritual relationship does not end because the body is no longer present and alive among us.

## Remembrances

With the end of the eleven-month period following burial, the most intensive rites that have permeated the lives of the mourners are brought to a close. However, the persistence and healing value of human memory necessitates some continuing form of recognition of a loss of a loved one. From this point on, the deceased are ritually remembered on five occasions during the year: They are the *yahrzeit*, as well as the four holidays when *yizkor* is said: Yom Kippur, Passover, Shavuot, and Shemini Atzeret. *Yahrzeit* and *yizkor* observance are later developments, probably dating from the Middle Ages. *Yahrzeit* is a Yiddish word of German origin, and Jews didn't speak Yiddish until the latter sixteenth to early seventeenth century, for the most part.

On the day of the *yahrzeit*, a memorial candle ought to be lit, charitable acts should be performed, and Jewish study should be included. Some people have even fasted on the *yahrzeit* of one's parents. They also visit the grave site and recite Psalms such as the ones often recited at an unveiling: Psalms 8, 19, 23, 46, 104, 120, 139, 146.

Beginning in the late nineteenth century, *yahrzeit* calendars were printed in Israel, Europe, and the United States.

While the *yahrzeit* falls on the same day according to the Jewish calendar, its secular date varies from year to year. Contact your rabbi or chaplain for help in calculating the dates. The *yahrzeit* remains an important point of contact with Jewish tradition, even for Jewish people who may not be observant in other areas of Jewish life.

## Leon Wieseltier's Kaddish Experience

A recent work about Kaddish is the highly acclaimed book *Kaddish* by Leon Wieseltier (published in 1998 by Knopf). When Leon Wieseltier's father died, Leon undertook to recite the Mourner's Kaddish at public worship three times a day. He did so for eleven months.

Wieseltier tells the story of the eleven months of saying Kaddish and of all his studies about Kaddish during those eleven months. The author reflects upon the great issues of life and death considered through the prisms of memory and of grief. Wieseltier enters into a dialogue with the great Judaic intellects of the ages whom he knows as companions. The result is a profound work not merely about Judaism but of Judaism.

Wieseltier enlists erudition to give comfort to the soul. He voices a controlled despair and restraint by saying Kaddish and by studying comments made about Kaddish by Jews over the period of many centuries.

Regarding the constancy of the author's rendition of Kaddish three times a day in a *minyan*, he writes that his unexpected fidelity to this obscure and arduous practice turned a season of sorrow into a season of soul renovation. Raised in a traditional Jewish home, Wieseltier moved away from religious observance as an adult. "Why," a friend asked, "did he choose to say Kaddish?" His answer is straightforward and compelling:

Because it is my duty to my father. Because it is my duty to religion. ... Because it would be harder for me not to say Kaddish. I would despise myself. Because the fulfillment of my duty leaves my thoughts about my father unimpeded by regret and undistorted by guilt.

Wieseltier establishes close bonds with the mourners in his synagogue. He is forever on the run between his office and the synagogue, not only because he is saying Kaddish, but *because there are other mourners to whom he feels obligated.* Similarly there is always someone else at the synagogue ready to make phone calls to gather a *minyan* so that Wieseltier can say Kaddish. Newcomers who appear on the scene are warmly welcomed whatever their background. Wieseltier writes:

The Rabbi introduces me to two men. They are brothers and they buried their father this morning. They have come to say Kaddish but they are not familiar with the words and the customs of the prayer. The Rabbi asks me to help. Soon it is time to recite the Kaddish. The brothers rise with me.
They read a transliteration of the prayer: "We are the dunces," one of them says. "No," I reply, "the dunces are the ones who don't try." As I watched the brothers struggle with the transliterated prayer, I admired them. The sounds that they uttered made no sense to them but there was so much fidelity, so much humility, in their gibberish.

Eleven months is a long time. On some mornings, Wieseltier struggles to rise at an early morning hour to go to the synagogue. As his eleven months of saying Kaddish enters the final stretch, he is frightened at the prospect of finishing. "As the end of the Kaddish nears," he states openly, "I am scared." And he explains why.

For as long as I have been organizing my life around the Kaddish, I have been organizing my life around my father.

10

When Kaddish is over, he will be gone. My strict observance of the year of mourning has had a consequence of delaying the return of a normal life. I have lived in a state of suspension, shielded from a fatherless world by a father-full practice. The Jewish way of mourning has turned an absence into a presence.

At times during the eleven months, Wieseltier wonders why he is saying Kaddish. He is making a dedicated effort to say Kaddish even though he never made that kind of effort to see his father when he was alive. Wieseltier affirms, "*Our fathers did not have the authority to ask this of us but our religion does.*" He is saying Kaddish to help himself to deal with the impact that his grieving has on him. He continues to say Kaddish for the year.

Wieseltier, a great writer, has expressed himself very well regarding the Kaddish. You will find, as I have already found, that the people whose words you are about to read have also expressed themselves well about the impact of the Kaddish on them. They speak from the heart in a way that can move you.

# II.

## THE IMPACT OF GRIEVING AND THE IMPORTANCE OF SAYING KADDISH: TEN VOICES

### Belonging, Behaving, Perhaps Even Believing

By Irving Berman

Before my father's death, my daily worship was nonexistent. My attendance at synagogue fell into the category of yearly. When I wished the clergy a good year, it was because, outside of a wedding or Bar Mitzvah, that was the next time I was likely to see them.

After the Shiva period ended, I was faced with living up to the commitment I had made to my father to say Kaddish for him. The reading of the Kaddish at three services each day seemed like a chore that was monumental. The first time I attended the morning service, I had little knowledge of what lay ahead. I was "doing this" for my dad. That first morning I was greeted by some of the "regulars" and found I had gained admittance to a club that none of us had wanted to join. My Hebrew skills were "rusty" to say the least. I was happy just to know what page we were on and when to stand and sit. For the next eleven months, and the first time in my adult life, my religion was to become a conscious part of my daily regimen.

As the days went by, I began to understand the purpose of the Kaddish service and feel its effect on me. I thought about my father every day. I began and ended my day with

13

a peaceful meditation and "conversation" with my God. I took time, not only for my father, but also for myself. Some of the mystery surrounding prayers, holidays, and traditions began to disappear. I met with other Jews who were attending services, out of necessity or by choice. I even found my "barely used" *t'fillin* [phylacteries] and began using them. I felt the healing process begin, and found that I was gaining a new and personal relationship with my religion. What had started out as a chore had become a satisfying task. What was once something I did for my father was now something I did for the two of us.

During the course of the eleven months, the members of the "club" changed. Each of us gained as much as we wanted. My Hebrew reading skills improved so that I was able to keep up with the service. I celebrated holidays and attended services that I had not participated in since I was a child. I even attended some services that I had never heard of before. My effort to fulfill my daily Kaddish obligations took so much of my time and energy, and I did not realize how soothing an impact it was having on me. The eleven months that at first seemed like an eternity passed in the blink of an eye. The loss that I felt I would never get over resulted in a life experience I now look at with a sense of pride. I learned a tremendous amount about my religion, met some wonderful people and found out a lot about myself. The last day, after saying my final required Kaddish, I stood on the *bimah* and led Maariv, the evening service. I was now doing it for me.

The Kaddish experience acted not only as a healing exercise, but a strengthening bond between myself, my father, my grandfather and those who preceded them. I am more aware that there is more to being Jewish than Bris [ritual circumcision of boys at age of eight days], Bar Mitzvah, and burial. A great deal is available in between, if we take the time to look for it.

# Renewing, Reconnecting, Re-entering
## By Gail Raminick

My background and knowledge of Judaism has always been unimpressive and yet I have always felt very strongly about being Jewish and about the impact of our ancestors on the world. When my father died, I said Kaddish at home with my husband, Shel. I knew that would be fine with my father. And I knew that where I prayed would not be important to my father, or, in fact, if I prayed. My father knew how much Shel and I loved him.

After Shel's death, I went to the synagogue where we belonged, to say Kaddish in the evening. The service, mainly in English, was a very beautiful and moving one that was right for me at that time. My older son was attending services at Adat Shalom, and we both tried each other's places. They didn't work for us. He wasn't comfortable at my synagogue and I wasn't comfortable here. I stopped going to my synagogue after the first month. There were very few people at their evening service, and there was no morning service. Something that I needed just wasn't there!

At that time, Rabbi Yoskowitz said, "Gail, come to our services here, once or twice a week. Just give it a try and see if it helps you." So I came once or twice a week for a couple of weeks and then the once or twice a week became every day before work and I started to feel that I wanted to be here on Sunday, too. I don't know what draws me here, and I don't know what draws me to the cemetery on a weekly basis either. I just feel a magnetic pull, and I do what it leads me to do. For a reason that I don't really understand, I feel better

15

being here. I don't read a word of Hebrew and can't always find where we are in the service. Some days I listen and read, and I see and hear only empty words. Some days those words are very meaningful to me. When I recite the words of the Kaddish, I think of my husband. I feel that this is something that I can do for him, for me and for us. Starting my day here gives me purpose. When I read the prayers and Psalms, I am looking for a spirituality that I need very much in my life. Shel had that spirituality. He never blamed God or anyone for his illness and always said, "It's the luck of the draw." He believed in God and he believed in us.

This has also become the place where I have re-entered the world without my husband. He will always be with me, but I have to learn to live as an "I" instead of a "we." Being in this accepting environment has been a good place to start. The friendships that I have made here are very important to me. Everyone cares about each other. We joke about our assigned seating, our attendance records, and sometimes we share a day that is harder than usual. We are all living with a hole in our lives and in our hearts. Some of our situations are easier to accept and rationalize than others, but we all have to manage. One of the women that I met here at Adat Shalom's morning service said, "Gail, when we started coming to say Kaddish, we were broken people. Now we are mending." Perhaps the words of the Kaddish do have a power to heal.

At the beginning I didn't know if I wanted to live without my husband. I just wanted to be with him. I still want to be with him somewhere, in some way, but the words from Psalm 30 on page 114 of the prayer book began to sink into my being. One line reads, "What profit is there in my death, when I go down to the grave? Shall the dust praise Thee? Shall it declare Thy truth?"

I'm not sure what my truth is, but I know that I want to believe in God and in something that is beyond what is here. I also want to live the rest of my life in a way that will honor Shel and me.

# Pulled Up and Pulled In
By Bill Graham

Ten months ago, our seventeen-year-old daughter, Alex, died of cancer. We had no regrets, as we did everything that could be done to save her life. We had no guilt, no anger and we were at peace.

Statistically I am significantly different from most members of the congregation. I keep kosher at home and out, virtually never miss Shabbat services, and lay *t'fillin* six days per week. Except for the period that our daughter was sick, I attended morning services once a week to help to assure that there would be a *minyan* so that others could say Kaddish. Saying Kaddish certainly hasn't been a life-changing event.

My first experience of saying Kaddish occurred nine years ago when my father died. He was a *mensch* [a gentleman], but not a spiritual person, and he was not Jewish. When a Jew mourns for a non-Jew, there are several opinions. Generally the process ends up being a compromise among the various siblings. I chose to be with my relatives until the funeral and then to say Kaddish at my synagogue for the *Shloshim* only.

After our daughter died, coming to morning services and saying Kaddish was the most natural thing for me to do. It was a way to honor her memory and, more importantly, it was a way for me to reaffirm my faith in God. Depending upon which Rabbi you ask, one should say Kaddish for just the thirty-day *Shloshim* period or for the full eleven months, as we chose to do. I have to be frank with you, I dreaded the thought of having to get up at 6:30 every weekday morning, and be at the synagogue by 7:30 on weekdays, and be committed to this discipline for eleven months. For thirteen months, I was doing everything that I could to save Alex's life and to make her life more normal. When Alex died, I lost a great deal of interest in life. Saying Kaddish took me out of the house and enabled me to be around old friends and to meet new friends.

Initially on days when the Torah was read, I just wanted to sit in my seat and not participate. Slowly our cantor urged me to participate by taking out and returning the Torah or by serving as *hagbah* [the person who raises the Torah from the Reading Table after the public reading] and then by receiving an *aliyah*. It could be likened to a very subtle pulling-up ceremony after one completes the *Shiva* period. It was one of the many small steps in returning from my daughter's grave to life. By saying Kaddish for the full eleven months, I avoided the potential for relapsing into seclusion and feeling alone.

Although I know modern Hebrew very well, I find the Aramaic of the Kaddish difficult to enunciate. The Kaddish d'Rabbanan (the Rabbis' Kaddish) is particularly difficult to enunciate, but, as my Rabbi says, "There is something special about the Aramaic that has precluded it from ever being translated into a more modern Hebrew." I agree.

If you ever see me at services, you'll notice that I tend to arrive late and have the *spilkas*, an edginess. I tend to find the Small Chapel too warm, so I get up, stand by the window a lot, and almost never stay for breakfast. I miss Alex terribly, but I accept her death as part of the human condition. It's part of the "deal." I am at peace during Kaddish; I feel as if I am a *tallit* [a prayer shawl] and I am wrapping myself around her, giving her comfort. In reality, I know that she is the one that is giving me comfort.

In closing, I say Kaddish as a means of honoring our

daughter and gaining comfort, but, most of all, reaffirming my faith in God. It is my faith that has given me the strength these past two years. If it were not for my faith in God, I would never have been able to handle this tragedy.

I have to admit that I'm beginning to have a panic attack. Kaddish will end in a month; I want it to last longer. However, eleven months is enough to say Kaddish. I have a lifetime to cherish the memories and will always have a special place in my heart for Alex.

# Friends in the Small Chapel

By Susie Graham

Initially Kaddish was a form of respect for my daughter. Ultimately, the final respect. It was hard, at first, to get up so early each morning; the truth is, it was much easier to be in bed and hide. But there was a strong current pulling me along. Throughout my journey over the last nine and a half months, saying the Kaddish has become my salvation. Most of the time, I'm not so sure what I am saying. When I can risk losing my place, I glance over at the English. It's interesting how the Kaddish prayer has nothing to do with death, but rather with praising God. And, in praising God, I think I reaffirm my belief in God at a time when it is so easy to lose faith and certainly question life and everything I once thought to be true. I now ask the question, "What will I do when Kaddish is no longer required of me?"

Saying Kaddish each morning has also somehow connected me with the past. The repetition . . . I think of my ancestors repeating the same prayers as I do now. I generally come to the morning service, Shaharit, so that not only am I saying Kaddish, but also observing an eleven-month period of the Jewish calendar! How much I've absorbed! Each morning is the same, yet so different—different people, people also suffering a loss, people remembering a loved one. Celebrations of Bar and Bat Mitzvah. A metaphor for life.

What a learning experience! I've brushed up on my Hebrew. I delight in the melodies. I can follow the service. I actually think of one day leading the service. I help a new

20

friend when she's lost her place. She's lost her husband. She relies on me. Life cycles. Unspoken words. Grief abounds. How close I've become to the Torah, both physically and spiritually. Sometimes I flip through the *siddur* and read Psalms. They console me.

In our large sanctuary on Shabbat morning, interestingly enough, I feel more secluded. My friends are not close to me, as they are in the small chapel. They sit in different sections of the sanctuary, some very far away. It is not as comfortable for me to stand up. Is everyone looking at me? Do they feel sorry for me? I stand with pride as I recite those age-old words.

I am a member of a very prestigious club that I did not choose. My comrades have all been wounded. They acknowledge me with a sweet smile. They understand how fragile life is. They understand my pain as I do theirs. They comfort me as the words of the Kaddish do. I am at peace.

# Stronger Than Death

By Shoshana Wolok

My dear mother died in 1989. She was ninety-one years old, so there was not the anguish one feels when a child or sparkling young person dies. But a beloved mother is never old enough to die. I had loved and respected her all my life, and my heart was sore.

With this sore heart, I entered the daily chapel to begin a twice-a-day prayer regimen for eleven months. Rising to recite Kaddish gave me some way to express my love for my mother and to receive comfort. I soon saw this act as a way of bearing witness that **love is as strong as death** (Song of Songs 8:6).

It was soon apparent which individuals were coming to observe *yahrzeit* and which Kaddish. Praying together and sharing breakfast together day after day created a special bond. Each new Kaddish-observer was welcomed quietly and warmly. It finally seemed to me that the Kaddish group may well be the first and most durable support group in history.

But there were older men, retired men, who came morning after morning, who were observing neither Kaddish nor *yahrzeit*. They simply loved a program of daily prayer and felt needed (something often lost in retirement) to make sure that there was a *minyan*. I then remembered that, growing up, I had seen my father, *z"l* [abbreviation for Zichrono Livrachah, may his memory be for a blessing], every morning put on his *tallit* and *t'fillin* and recite the morning prayers. When he was home at late afternoon, he would go to the east wall, facing

22

Jerusalem, and recite the afternoon and evening prayers, *Minhah* and *Maariv* (he knew the prayers by heart). It was clear that being part of a "kingdom of priests" naturally involved a regimen of daily prayer.

Before Sukkot my husband and I flew to Israel for a six-week visit with our daughter, son-in-law, and three Israeli grandchildren. My Kaddish observance continued at the neighborhood Conservative Synagogue. In my heart, I said to my mother, "I am observing Kaddish for you in Yerushalayim. This is a great honor for you."

A few more months passed. The one thing that had seemed odd was that, in the hours of pain, we were reciting an ode of adoration to God. But one morning, as I was looking at the rising sun, the thought came to me, "How could God be so good to me as to give me such a wonderful mother, this wise and beautiful woman, this living personification of selfless love to her children, and a living example of the saintly person?" And then I understood that the recitation of Kaddish is an ode of Thanksgiving and totally appropriate.

Kaddish means that, when the Shiva and the condolence calls are over—when the house becomes silent, and the loss is sharp and intense—a Jew need not suffer alone. Comfort, fellowship, and emotional support are as close as the nearest synagogue.

# Watching My Father Say Kaddish

By David W. Schostak

My thoughts about the positive impact of the age-old tradition of reciting the Kaddish in memory of our loved ones are neither original nor out of the ordinary, but they are deeply personal.

I have two very vivid, yet very different experiences with saying Kaddish. The first occurred not as a direct result of my saying Kaddish, but had a permanent impact on my life. On May 5, 1970, seven months to the day before my Bar Mitzvah, my paternal grandfather passed away. My father had been raised in a Reform house, but with my mother, who chose to send us to Hillel Day School and who affiliated with the Conservative Movement, he chose to say Kaddish every morning and evening for the eleven months.

I don't know how it started, but my brothers and I began to go with my father every morning to Adat Shalom to say Kaddish with him. It became a morning ritual. He would wake us up, we would go to *shul* [synagogue] and then he would drop us off at Hillel Day School after services. Not only did it permanently enhance the bond among my brothers, our father, and me; it also contributed to our ability, even thirty years later, to lead the Shacharit service in the morning.

Even more interesting are permanent memories of that year and the links that were forged with the other members of the daily *minyan* who were also saying Kaddish. To this day, when I see those members, I fondly reflect back on the time that we spent together. When I occasionally read or hear of their passing, it harkens me once more again to the days that we used to go to *shul* with my father for him to say Kaddish for his father.

Unfortunately, twenty-six years later, almost to the day, my wife and I lost a child. And there again I found myself with the *need*, not just the obligation, to say Kaddish.

That experience was very much different from the one I had twenty-six years earlier with my father, because shortly after *shivah*, we traveled to Israel for a previously planned trip for a joyous occasion, a *simcha*, the Bat Mitzvah of our niece. As a result, I spent all of *shloshim*, bouncing from one *shul* to the next, all over the State of Israel—sometimes in a Conservative setting, sometimes in an Orthodox setting, at other times in a Sephardic *shul*, but rarely in the same place twice.

Although I was clearly a stranger in each one of those synagogues, and literate in Hebrew, I was generally ignorant of their individual cultures and styles. Yet, I felt the immediate overwhelming warmth from all of the congregants, because they knew that I, too, was there to say Kaddish. I thought back to the time that I spent with my father when he was saying Kaddish. I remembered the bond that I had built with people that had become our very close friends as a result of that experience together. I realized that here I was with Jews from all over the world in Israel whom I did not know and never saw before and would never see again—but that same bond immediately existed when we said Kaddish together.

As a result of these two very different, yet similar experiences, I am convinced that it is God's infinite wisdom that mourners spend that time together. It not only helps their mourning and their healing, but builds lifelong relationships which enables everyone in mourning to gain something positive from their loss.

# Saying Kaddish as the Anger Fades

By George Max Saiger

My name is George Saiger. I was blessed to have both my parents alive until I was fifty years old. One thing that I came to believe with ever greater certainty as I got older was that I did not intend to say Kaddish for my parents every day for a year when it came time for them to die. I had long developed the habit of going to *shul* every Shabbat and Yom Tov. It was my expectation to say the Kaddish when, and only when, I was in *shul* anyway. Anything more seemed both onerous and meaningless, a deadly combination.

Then, one August evening, my mother died. Shiva was difficult for me. It was a mix of pain, tears, comfort, reflection, and boredom. We had a *minyan* in my house twice every day, as is the custom of my congregation. I was touched by the number of people who came to help make a *minyan*. At the end of it, the Rabbi stayed after the last morning service. "Put your shoes on," he said. "We are going for a walk around the block." I took off the bedroom slippers I had worn all week and went out for the first time. It was a nice summer day, perfect for a walk, perfect for getting back into my regular life. We talked about a variety of things, the Rabbi and I, including, I now remember, the idea that I should let the big Shiva candle burn itself out, letting Mother's soul linger in the house a bit longer. Then he left. At the door, he said, "*Minyan* at the *shul* this afternoon is at 6:05. See you then." Until that moment, I had not considered it—just as he had not considered that I wouldn't be there. I didn't see how I could respond

26

to his warm support by starting a discussion about why I did not intend to go.

So I went. It was an odd experience. People greeted me with expressions of support, but I felt somewhat trapped by them and by the tradition. I remember feeling that they were welcoming me into the fellowship of the damned. And they were to be my *hevra* (fellow travelers) for a while. That first month, the time of *sh'loshim*, I felt mostly angry while I was in *shul*. I was angry that my mother was dead. I was angry that my prayers, and those of so many family and friends, for her recovery were not answered. I was angry that I suddenly had the burden of care of my ninety-two-year-old father. The icing on that bitter cake was my obligation to stand at the *ammud* (lecturn), leading the congregation in prayers. Thus I was required to respond to my situation by intoning, over and over: "*Yitgadal v'yitkadash Sh'mei rabbah* . . . Magnified and sanctified is His great name." Inside I raged: "You can make me stand here. You can make me say these words. But You cannot make me accept that there is something right and holy about my mother being dead!"

I don't know when the anger began to fade. My last *hiyyuv* (obligation) as a mourner in *sh'loshim* was at *minchah* (the afternoon service), just before the beginning of Rosh HaShanah. I got there a few minutes late, and they held up that service, with hundreds of people there instead of the usual fifteen or twenty, waiting for me to lead them. "Hurry up, George, move it!" somebody said. I was touched—and maybe that's when I started to get less angry. Or maybe rage was just starting to wear thin already.

As autumn grew into winter, I found myself more welcoming of this new daily routine. I would often reflect about Mother during services, remembering this or that, and rather enjoying it. New mourners came, and now it was my turn to welcome them. Friendships grew out of that time. One, with Alan R., who started saying Kaddish about two months after I did, has continued ever since. We would negotiate which of us

27

would lead which service and how long to wait for a *minyan*, or we'd just chat about nothing in particular while waiting.

In time this became routinized, just something I did every day. I decided that I needed to make it again become a conscious decision, so I purposely skipped a day here or there. It made me feel good, feel that I was still in control of my life. Consciously I had that mischievous good feeling on the mornings when I lay in bed an hour longer. Unconsciously it was even more important on those mornings when I did attend the *minyan*.

As spring came, it became clearer that this, too, would end. I couldn't bear to skip on purpose anymore, because there were so few days left in which I would have these minutes dedicated to my mother, *aleha hashalom* (may she be at peace). That addendum to her name had gradually crept into my feeling about her. It meant that Mother was now a memory, a soul which lingered ever more tentatively around the Kaddish, around the *minyan*, around my life.

And then it was over. I stood at the *ammud* for a while in silence after that last Kaddish.

"Hey, George," someone said, "the service is over. What's with you?"

"It was my last time," I answered.

There is an epilogue. Mother had died on *Rosh Hodesh Elul* [the first day of the Hebrew month of Elul]. I attended daily *minyan* for a while longer after my eleven months were over, no longer saying Kaddish. After the *yahrtzeit*, the special Psalm for *Elul*, "L 'David HaShem Ori" (Psalm XXVII) was added, to be recited twice daily during the month before and the month after Rosh HaShanah. One verse jumped out at me, one I hadn't noticed during *Elul* a year earlier, when I was just starting this journey. "For my father and my mother have left me, and God will gather me in."

Daddy died a few years later, also in early *Elul*. This verse has become something of my ongoing Kaddish for them ever since.

# Remembering

By David Techner,
Ira Kaufman Funeral Home


In Melvindale, some skinhead kids had done some particular damage, and I was asked to go into the high school and address an assembly. At the time, I was president of the Michigan Funeral Directors Assembly, and happened to be the only Jew in the association.

During the question and answer session, a student came to the microphone and very respectfully asked this question: "Mr. Techner, I think you have a lot of guts to come here after this incident in this community and I appreciate your being here. But there is one thing I really would like to know. Why can't Jews forget the Holocaust?"

I was stunned by the question, although I didn't show it. It was a very thoughtful question based upon the discussion to that point. And I said to him, "Could you please repeat the question?" Now I must tell you that you could hear a pin drop when he asked the question. I replied: "Do you know anything about Judaism?" He said, "No, I don't." I asked if he ever had taken any comparative religion classes. And he said, "No, I have not." And I said, "Let me tell you a little bit about Judaism." And I proceeded to talk about Kaddish, about *Kibud Hamet* (the respect of the dead), about *Yizkor*, the synagogue services held four times during the year when the deceased family members and friends are remembered, about *Yahrzeit*, the Hebrew date of the death of family and friends on which we say prayers for the souls of our departed. We go to services; we say Kaddish. On the four days during the course of the year, we have *Yizkor*. I looked at him and I said: "You see, it's not just the Holocaust; Jews don't forget about anybody."

Remembering our collective history and the histories of people whom we know is truly the hallmark of who we are as a people. To me, remembering our dead by saying Kaddish is one of the great beauties of being a Jew. Through the Kaddish Minyan, we become acquainted with other people who have suffered a similar loss. When we say the Kaddish together we are uplifted even as we give other Kaddish sayers our support.

# Avenues of Growth

By Rabbi Boruch E. Levin,
Hebrew Memorial Chapel

We know the importance of *mesorah* or "tradition" in our religion. It is interesting for me to see the deep conviction of people regarding this *mitzvah* of saying Kaddish. Jews who are otherwise detached from other areas of Jewish life have accepted upon themselves the responsibility of reciting the Kaddish for their departed loved ones. Although many of these mourners don't realize the rich heritage and importance of Kaddish, they still have this almost inborn feeling that urges them to recite the Kaddish in honor of the deceased. This feeling comes from an innate spark of *Yiddishkeit* that God has implanted in all of us. It reminds me of the Passover Seder in which most Jews participate, although their commitment to traditional Judaism might be minimal. It gives me personal strength when I realize how God put these rituals into our lives as guideposts and firm stepping stones in our journey through life.

I also find strength in the fact that God gives survivors not only a path of consolation through the observance of Shiva and in mourning rituals, but also an avenue of growth. We all know that there is a finality in death. A monument which describes the deceased's good deeds attests to that finality, by being etched in stone. Nothing changes, potential is nil and growth impossible—no additional *mitzvot*, no epitaphs changed. But the Kaddish sends its message—"*Yitgadal v'yitkadash shmay rabaw*—may God's great name be magnified and sanctified."

"By whom?" we should ask. "By us," must be the answer. Only if we, the survivors, reflect on the life that has passed, the parent that has taught, the link in our Jewish history that is now us, can we make some sense of what we are reciting. We are forced to ponder what legacy we received and maybe more importantly what legacy *we* will transmit. Personal growth, therefore, begs to be addressed head on—with the goal being "May God's great name be magnified and sanctified." God obviously does not need us to magnify and sanctify His name. Rather God has allowed us to do so to elevate our lives for our betterment, and for the betterment of all humanity. The Kaddish proclamation gives us direction—and therefore consolation. Death brought on unattachment. Kaddish brings on attachment—a deep feeling of belonging—to the past, present and future, to this golden chain that we call tradition or *mesorah* in our religion.

God in His infinite wisdom has given us Jews this precious practice of saying Kaddish, a practice which is so powerful and meaningful. The final ability to do one more concrete thing for Mom or Dad is most gratifying. It even gives the living a connection with the dead. Although death is final, it isn't as brutal. We don't feel as helpless.

# Comfort and Tranquility

By Jonathan M. Dorfman,
Dorfman Funeral Directors

As a practicing Jewish funeral director and psychologist for the past ten years, I have had the opportunity to assist families through one of the most difficult experiences in their lives. In dealing with these families and trying to comfort them and direct them on the path toward healing, I have found the Kaddish to be a very resourceful tool.

Judaism affords many unique and creative insights into death and mourning. It teaches that following the death of a loved one it is appropriate to say Kaddish for a period of eleven months, less one day, beginning from the date of death. The Kaddish gives the mourners guidance and hope in the face of great despair. I personally feel it teaches individuals to be strong, even when faced with a devastating loss. The prayer is traditionally said at the conclusion of the service after the lowering of the casket, which psychologically is one of the hardest aspects of the service. And during this emotionally draining period, the family and mourners and friends are standing side by side, shoulder to shoulder, and praising God's name. The beauty is not just in the words of the Kaddish but in the rhythm of the words. Saying it in the presence of others facilitates emotional healing (by outwardly expressing one's feelings and emotions). As a psychologist, I always say "grief shared is grief lessened," and it seems our ancient Tradition practices this insight. The Kaddish has helped our people from generation to generation and will continue to do so for generations to come.

In today's rapidly changing world, we need to seek comfort and tranquility in the stability of Tradition. Many people utilize Tradition only in times of great sorrow and duress. Fortunately, we have these customs to help to guide us during these difficult periods in our lives. We must again thank and praise God for supporting us and for granting us life, thus embracing the precious words of the Kaddish.

# III.

## COMMENTING, LEADING AND MEDITATING ON THE KADDISH

### Linear Translation and Commentary on the Mourner's Kaddish

By Rabbi Daniel Nevins

#### INTRODUCTION
#### Genre

There are three major genres of Jewish prayer: praise (שבח), petition (בקשה), and thanksgiving (הודאה). The latter two genres relate to the needs and experiences of people, whereas the first focuses on the sanctity of God. Praise-prayers seek to transport the person beyond his or her own needs, and as such, are the purest liturgical form.

The rabbis classed several praise-prayers in a special category called "matters of sanctity" (דברים שבקדושה). These liturgical selections include the call to prayer (ברכו), the section of the reader's Amidah called "Kedushah" (קדושה), and the Kaddish (קדיש). All of these prayers require a *minyan*, a quorum of ten Jews who constitute a miniature version of Israel. While individual meditation is a praiseworthy and even necessary element of a spiritual life, Judaism instructs us that the Creator's praise is most impactful when announced in public. This requirement has sustained many a synagogue, as Jews learn to seek one another out in their goal of spiritual transcendence.

These "matters of sanctity" are all recited responsively, with a call and response interplay between a leader and the congregation. Their purpose is to sanctify God's name in this world, even as Isaiah described the angels' unceasing song in heaven.

## Language

The words of the Kaddish are an amalgam of Hebrew and scholarly Jewish Aramaic, which was the language of Jewish Torah scholars in the early Talmudic era. The familiar cadence of the Kaddish derives from the reflexive grammatical form (*Ithpael* in Aramaic; *Hitpael* in Hebrew) shared by ten of its opening words. Thus, *Yitgadal, v'Yitkaddash* in the first paragraph, and *Yitbarach, v'Yishtabach, vYitpoar, v'Yitromam, v'Yitnasei, v'Yithadar, v'Yitaleh, v'Yithalal* in the third paragraph, are all reflexive verbs that are nearly synonyms for God's exalted stature.

Aside from the pleasing cadence of this string of verbs, there is a theological message in their grammar. Rather than directly praising God, we ask that God be praised—it would be presumptuous to assume that we ourselves can cause God to be great. Moreover, this prayer praises not God's essence, but God's name. There is therefore deep humility and reverence embedded in the very grammar and diction of the Kaddish.

## Origins

The origins and original function of the Kaddish are shrouded in mystery. Its kernel is clearly the Aramaic verse from the book of Daniel (2:20), "May His great name be blessed forever and ever," which has a Hebrew equivalent in Psalms 113:2. This phrase, which is reverently referred to throughout Talmudic literature, became the cornerstone for the various versions of the Kaddish, which originated in Palestine, and were developed further in Babylonia. The original use of the Kaddish had no connection to mourning; this association is first mentioned explicitly only in the thirteenth century. By that time, the legend of Rabbi Akiva saving a man's soul from perdition by teaching his son to recite Kaddish in synagogue had spread. This is apparently the ultimate cause for the medieval practice instituting קדיש יתום, the Mourner's (literally, orphan's) Kaddish. The Sephardic (and some Chasidic) traditions include in the first paragraph a request that God's redemption and  messiah be delivered (ויצמח פרקנה וקרב משיחה).

Great and holy[1] shall His[2] great name[3] be in the world that He created by His will![4]

May His kingdom be established by your life and in your days[5] and in the life of the entire House of Israel.[6] Now, and speedily,[7] and say "Amen!"[8]

יִתְגַּדַּל וְיִתְקַדַּשׁ שְׁמֵהּ רַבָּא בְּעָלְמָא דִּי בְרָא כִרְעוּתֵהּ וְיַמְלִיךְ מַלְכוּתֵהּ בְּחַיֵּיכוֹן וּבְיוֹמֵיכוֹן וּבְחַיֵּי דְכָל בֵּית יִשְׂרָאֵל בַּעֲגָלָא וּבִזְמַן קָרִיב וְאִמְרוּ : אָמֵן

**May His great name be blessed[9] forever and ever![10]**

יְהֵא שְׁמֵהּ רַבָּא מְבָרַךְ לְעָלַם וּלְעָלְמֵי עָלְמַיָּא

Blessed, acclaimed, glorified, elevated, raised high, beautified, exalted and praised[11] be the name of the Holy One, **blessed be He![12]**

יִתְבָּרַךְ וְיִשְׁתַּבַּח וְיִתְפָּאַר וְיִתְרוֹמַם וְיִתְנַשֵּׂא וְיִתְהַדָּר וְיִתְעַלֶּה וְיִתְהַלָּל שְׁמֵהּ דְּקוּדְשָׁא בְּרִיךְ הוּא

[God is] Beyond[13] all blessings, songs[14] praises and consolations that are said on earth, and say "Amen."

לְעֵלָּא מִן כָּל
בִּרְכָתָא וְשִׁירָתָא
תֻּשְׁבְּחָתָא וְנֶחֱמָתָא
דַּאֲמִירָן בְּעָלְמָא
וְאִמְרוּ : אָמֵן

May great peace come[15] from heaven and life for us and all Israel, and say "Amen."

יְהֵא שְׁלָמָא רַבָּא מִן שְׁמַיָּא
וְחַיִּים עָלֵינוּ וְעַל כָּל יִשְׂרָאֵל
וְאִמְרוּ : אָמֵן

May He Who makes peace above also make peace for us[16] and for all Israel, and say, "Amen."

עֹשֶׂה שָׁלוֹם בִּמְרוֹמָיו
הוּא יַעֲשֶׂה שָׁלוֹם
עָלֵינוּ וְעַל כָּל יִשְׂרָאֵל
וְאִמְרוּ : אָמֵן

—Mourner's Kaddish reprinted from
*Friday Night Alive!* © 1998 The Singlish Publication Society,
*www.singlishps.com.*

---

1. **Great and Holy**. Jewish theology balances two visions of God—transcendent and immanent. The transcendent vision of God—mighty, awesome, even frightening—is indicated by the first word, *Yitgadal* ("Great"). We often first think of God in terms of greatness, but Judaism seeks to move us to a more intimate relationship with God. The second word, *v'Yitkadash* (holy), is a source of connection between God and humans, for we are instructed to become holy via the commandments, even as God is known as The Holy One, Praised be He. This understanding of a God whom we can imitate is more immanent. Both modes of relating to God are necessary for a balanced Jewish perspective.
2. **His**. The masculine pronoun is here used to describe God, although the attributes of God alluded to in this prayer are alternately masculine and feminine in Jewish mystical theology.
3. **Great name**. We bless God's name but do not presume to comprehend or affect God's essence.

4. **In the world**. Isaiah envisioned the angels sanctifying God's name "in the upper heavens." Our task is to make this created realm a laboratory producing holiness, thereby affirming the worth of our existence.

5. **By your life and in your days**. Is this phrase redundant, or does each word contribute new meaning? The former phrase implies that the totality of our lives should function to sanctify God, but that is a very tall order. In fact, Rabbi Akiva is said to have died satisfied (despite his tortured end) that he had fulfilled the command to love God "with all your being." For most humans, the method to accomplish this goal is much more mundane: through daily decisions to live a life of goodness. Thus "in your days" may be a more accessible way to sanctify God "by your life."

6. **The entire House of Israel**. Never underestimate the significance of our collective service to God. This prayer may not be uttered without a *minyan*, in fulfillment of the verse "I shall be sanctified in the midst of the children of Israel." (Leviticus, 22:32) God is said to rejoice in our unity, and to bemoan our division. When our collective existence becomes a "*Kiddush HaShem*" (sanctification of God's name), the redemption will surely be near.

7. **Now and speedily**. The messianic yearning of the Kaddish first emerges with these words. No mere recitation, this is an urgent demand addressed to the congregation to transform the world.

8. **Say "Amen!"** The congregation affirms all that the reader has said with this response, which is an acronym for the Hebrew words אל מלך נאמן (God, the faithful king). The Kaddish is essentially a call and response prayer.

9. **May His great name be blessed**. This is the kernel of the Kaddish, based on Daniel 2:20 and Psalms 113:2. The Talmud and commentaries (Shabbat 119b) emphasize that this response should be said vigorously, either through intense concentration or through raising one's voice in praise of God. Mystics read significance into the seven words and twenty-eight letters of this phrase, seeing it as a pillar of creation (seven days) and a source of strength (from the word כח "strength," whose numerical value is 28).

10. **Forever and ever!** An alternative understanding, based on the commentary *Metzudat David*, would be from this lower world to the supernal realm. In other words, may our humble praise resound across the heavens! The Jewish mystical tradition understands human actions on earth as impacting the heavenly realms beyond our comprehension.

11. **. . . and praised**. This concludes a string of eight verbs (in the reflexive grammatical form) praising God. Each word brings its own nuance

39

but as a group they form a doxology, or powerful paean of praise. Added to the first two words of the Kaddish, we have ten verbs of praise, corresponding to the ten mystical *sefirot* or dimensions of God's essence that are discernible to humans.

12. **Blessed be He!** This phrase is said by the reader and then repeated by the congregation. In some congregations, the response is "Amen."

13. **Beyond**. During the ten days of repentance from Rosh HaShannah through Yom Kippur, this phrase is replaced with לעלא לעלא מכל, "over and beyond all," because during this time we strive for an elevated spiritual sense even as God's sovereignty is more keenly apprehended.

14. **Blessings, songs**. In addition to being a prayer said by mourners, the Kaddish is used throughout the service to introduce or conclude various sections. This reference acknowledges that God is far greater than all of the praise that we utter in our liturgy.

15. **May great peace come**. Until this point, the Kaddish has offered pure praise of God. In a shift of genre, it now adds two Hebrew petitions asking for peace on earth.

16. **Also make peace for us**. This paragraph appears to repeat the message of the prior one, which also asked for peace. But while the former petition was oblique, asking "may peace come from heaven," the closing prayer is more insistent, asking that God intervene in the affairs of this world, sharing the heavenly peace with the people Israel during our lives. Nevertheless, the entire Kaddish prayer is extremely humble, never addressing God in the second person, and asking only for the most elevated of blessings, for peace.

# Leading the Kaddish: Impact on a Cantor

By Cantor Howard Glantz

As a young *chazzan* (cantor) just out of school, I remember feeling uncomfortable leading the Mourner's Kaddish at the daily *minyan* service with a quorum. After all, I was not a mourner, and I had vivid recollections of being urged to sit down in the chapel of my parents' *shul* as soon as the Mourner's Kaddish was announced in that only mourners stand for and say the Kaddish prayer in traditional circles.

The words were certainly familiar. Of all the liturgy in the *siddur* (prayer book) or *machzor* (prayer book for the High Holy Days), the Kaddish, in its various forms, is the most repeated text. The words rolled off my tongue as quickly as my telephone number and I enjoyed marking Shabbat and Holy Days with the traditional tunes and *nusach* (the traditional modes prescribed for chanting the liturgy). But somehow, leading people in a Mourner's Kaddish, I anticipated as being something very different.

Of course, I forged ahead performing this job requirement. Slowly and deliberately, I carefully enunciated each syllable of the Kaddish. As I became more and more accustomed to it, I viewed leading the Kaddish as a helpful task. With each person having a slightly different pace and pronunciation of this affirmation, I found that many could stay with the text easier having a leader to keep the pace steady and the words precise. Yes, it often struck me that I was not one of "them"—I had not experienced the obligation of saying the Mourner's Kaddish for a loved one; so I saw myself as being unqualified for even the simplest of tasks associated with death. Even less so was I appropriate to be the one making the final prayers by the grave or comforting the mourners.

Logic didn't really play in these more-than-fleeting insecure thoughts. I knew rationally that I could be effective and helpful without having had an immediate loss. As I grew to know my congregation more intimately, I had occasion to witness deaths of several people with whom I had shared meaningful times. I experienced these losses personally; still, I was not obligated to Kaddish.

Then, almost three years ago, I received the news of my father's *z"l* death while enjoying a Caribbean cruise with my wife—the first vacation we had taken alone since the birth of our children. Being unable to leave the ship for three more days, the postponing of the funeral and the making of travel arrangements turned out to be no small feat. Suddenly I became aware of the wisdom in our heritage when I recalled the laws pertaining to the Onen (one whose immediate relative has died but whose funeral has not yet taken place). Despite this knowledge that I had no obligation to wear *tefillin* or to pray publicly, the feeling of being stranded drew me to the Friday evening service on the ship. When the Mourner's Kaddish was announced, I knew that I had to sit. Once I had seen to it that my father's *z"l* (of blessed memory) was resting properly could I be asked to affirm God's greatness in this awesome manner.

I remember practicing this moment in my mind and wondering if by some magic I was going to be "qualified" now. From that first Kaddish at the grave to the last Kaddish said at the *mincha* service eleven months from the date of burial, I had the strong feeling that I was being gradually strengthened through the experience and being assured that, in time, with God's help, it would be okay.

And today, while there are sad moments and memories

in time, it is okay. I am once again not obligated to say the Mourner's Kaddish daily. I thought that this discomfort of leading the congregation would be gone. However, it is more difficult, in that I can't help but remember what it was like for me during those eleven months.

# A Therapist's Response to Saying Kaddish

By Ruby E. Kushner, ACSW

As I write this, my father's passing is very recent, so the following is my conscious awareness as of now. The "now" is the amplified immediacy.

My mother's death five years ago propelled me into being my father's caretaker. Death transforms the living, and I grew in strength and patience, and, I hope kindness and generosity as I accepted the obligation.

I have been a psychotherapist for over twenty-five years, and worked with people of many faiths, from Catholics to Wiccans. I am no expert on comparative religions, but I am not aware of another faith, besides Judaism, that has so much reality and healing offered in its ritual as a way to cope with loss. Most religions have no healing ritual that extends beyond the funeral. The absence of form leaves people feeling confused, uneasy, adrift. They often have no experience with death and assume their reactions are abnormal. The eleven months of mourning for a Jewish parent, or the thirty days for a spouse, offer very realistic options, giving the mourner a way to adjust to the loss.

From a clinical point of view, there are two diagnostic categories: "brief depressive reaction" is an adjustment disorder with depressed mood; "prolonged depressive reactions" implies dysfunction. Judaism's prescription for mourning speaks to the first of these two, acknowledging the reality of time to adjust.

An antidote to depression is performing the required rituals. Thus, I have chosen to be at services at least once a day to say the Mourner's Kaddish. The observance and the physical effort of showing up at a specific time and place are concrete ways to counteract the sadness of my loss and to give my grief somewhere to go and something to do.

Other daily morning prayers, besides the Kaddish, evoke gratitude in me. They renew my appreciation for opening my eyes in the morning, for God's gifts to me of my parents, as well as for others who have blessed my life with their presence.

As I say the Kaddish, my mind uncovers more reasons to appreciate what my parents did for me. When I feel sad as I grieve for my parents' physical absence, the Kaddish lets me keep the sadness for now. In the future, I anticipate that the Kaddish will annually and seasonally allow for revisiting my losses.

The Kaddish offers me satisfaction as I recognize that I am saying Kaddish for my father just as he did for his. My joining in the Kaddish Minyan is a way to link me to my father and to his generation. Special to me are the familiar faces at the daily services, and the new faces who become part of the inner circle of those saying Kaddish, their nods, their greetings, their voices that join with mine when we say the Kaddish.

The support of the clergy is consoling as they invite me to share the story of my life. They, through their voices, words and dignity, give the Kaddish Minyan experience greater comfort and consolation for me.

Saying the Kaddish helps me to take care of my soul. The words and the rhythm of the Kaddish are a part of my healing as I give my grief somewhere to go and something to do in the process of mending my broken heart.

# Seven Dimensions of the Kaddish Minyan: A "Jewish Clinical" Look

By Rabbi Simkha Y. Weintraub, CSW

The Kaddish Minyan is one of the richest, soundest structures for the griefwork of bereaved individuals and families, a remarkable confluence of religious observance, spiritual impact, psychological insight, and emotional depth. It offers a range of resources, whose sum is more than simply the total of the parts. Consider these seven dimensions:

**A Place:** The loss of a close one pulls the rug out from under one's feet. A bereaved person may feel emotionally homeless, psychologically disoriented, and/or unwilling or unable to return easily to familiar contexts of life (home, work, social settings) that may once have been so comforting and effortless. The Kaddish Minyan, which often meets in a relatively intimate "daily chapel" of a synagogue, provides a place designated, among other central purposes, for the mourner. The world at large may urge one to "move on," to somehow return to one's former self, to an earlier and easier script—but in the place of the Kaddish Minyan it is critical to be touched by the past, and one is expected not only to remember but to reaffirm one's shifting but ongoing connection to the departed.

Recall how, in greeting the mourner in the days following the loss, Jewish practice suggests the blessing "May the *Makom* (literally "the Place," one traditional way of referring

46

to God) comfort you among all the mourners of Zion and Jerusalem." The Kaddish Minyan offers a sense of that Place.

**People:** After a loss, one natural reaction is to withdraw, to pull inwards, to buffer oneself against stimuli (including, but not only, painful or challenging stimuli) in one's vulnerable and exposed state. Over time, one gradually begins to let others in and to reach out to others, and the Kaddish Minyan offers the perfect cohort and context for this incremental re-opening. Some participate in the *minyan* simply out of a basic, general commitment to communal Jewish prayer, unrelated to loss, but others may be there to commemorate the annual *yahrzeit* of a beloved one, or to help ensure the quorum of ten, and some with a recent, gaping personal wound. Each requires the other for the community to somehow join in praising God, despite the profound hurts they have sustained and irreparable absences they endure.

**Perspectives, Purposes:** As time moves on, the stories of the other mourners and community members in the Kaddish Minyan can become a unique source of insight and reflection. Their experiences and insights may support and even inspire, and they may offer some very practical guidance (*Where can I donate his clothes? How can I attend an upcoming family wedding? How did you decide on the tombstone's wording? Etc.*). Reflected in the faces and words of others, one's own journey is enhanced and deepened, and certainly rendered more bearable and intelligible. The fellow travelers of the Kaddish Minyan may constitute an invaluable family for both grief and renewal, representing a chorus of related voices, a treasury of helpful ideas.

**A Pastor:** Very often, the rabbi, cantor, or *shammes* (sexton), or lay leaders committed to the *minyan*, become valuable pastoral and spiritual supports. They may serve as special listening ears or dependable shoulders, they may help with questions of ritual practice or theological issues, they may teach or guide, respond or model. On Monday and Thursday mornings, when the Torah is read, or on *Rosh Hodesh*/The New Moon, or around Jewish holidays, they may share helpful and inspiring *Divrei Torah*/Words of Torah. For many, drawing closer to the clergy "up there on the *bimah*" is part of a de-mystification of Jewish religious tradition and Jewish spiritual life, that opens doors previously shut.

**Prayer:** Loss and suffering have a muting effect on people. The Kaddish, is, of course, central to the *minyan*, and over the weeks and months, it becomes a shared mantra-like chant to help carry one forward in one's grief and mourning. But other prayers, psalms, and readings may also expand in their meaning and relevance, and open up as containers for deeply felt emotions, profound values, and fundamental beliefs. Certain tunes may emerge as particularly comforting; certain lines (for example, from psalms) may serve to express one's current state of spirit—hopeful, lonely, grateful, despairing, searching, etc. The experience of prayer—both communal and personal, fixed and spontaneous—may unfold as more accessible and more involving than before. At one and the same time, a mourner may develop a traditional repertoire *and* a highly individual voice of prayer.

**A Plan, a Path:** Loss leads so often to depression, which, in turn, is often manifest in a frozen state of inaction, a tendency to want to "stay under the blankets" and do little. To an extent, that inclination, that *need*, must be respected and indulged, but it can easily become maladaptive, compounding depression and misery. The commitment to challenge one's crippling sadness by joining a Kaddish Minyan may constitute a first step of re-empowering oneself, of embarking on a path, following a plan of re-entry. So much can seem uncertain, so many routines may appear meaningless—but the regular participation in a Kaddish Minyan counteracts purposelessness and gives one something to do, precisely when it feels that there is nothing one *can* do.

**Presence and Peace:** In the course of time, the Kaddish ritual enables one to integrate painful losses into one's life story—never to forget, but rather to increasingly draw on memory for its healing potential. What once may have triggered only great pain and emptiness now fosters a measure of solace and wholeness. Memory, at first a pointer to what is no longer, now feeds a sustaining vision of what was, and what can be. Like the very experience in a Kaddish Minyan, we realize that we are part of an eternal people, that all must cope with pain and loss, and all can reach, together, for hope and transcendence. We sense, we affirm, we pray: *God will bring peace, not only to me/us, but to All: Amen.*

---

Readers may be interested in an essay by Dr. Saul Scheidlinger, "The Minyan as a Psychological Support System," which appeared in the August 1997 *Psychoanalytic Review* (84, 4).—SYW

# Meditations

### The Tradition of the Kaddish

The origins of the Kaddish are mysterious; angels are said to have brought it down from heaven. . . .

It possesses wonderful power. Truly, if there is any bond strong enough to chain heaven to earth, it is this prayer. It keeps the living together, and forms a bridge to the mysterious realm of the dead. One might almost say that this prayer is the . . . guardian of the people by whom alone it is uttered; therein lies the warrant of its continuance. Can a people disappear and be annihilated so long as a child remembers its parents?

Because this prayer does not acknowledge death, because it permits the blossom, which has fallen from the tree of humankind, to flower and develop again in the human heart, therefore it possesses sanctifying power.

(Excerpted from the *Gates of Prayer*,
copyrighted by the Central Conference of
American Rabbis and reprinted by permission.)

### The Kaddish

The Kaddish is not a prayer for the dead, but a mandate to the living. It bids us rise above our sorrow, and fixes our view upon the welfare of humanity. It lifts our hope and directs our vision to a day when all shall at last inhabit the earth as children of the one God, when justice shall reign supreme, in peace.

—Richard C. Hertz

"The loving kindness which we show to the departed is the ultimate form of loving kindness" (Rashi).

One of the most tender examples of such loving kindness is the recitation of the Mourner's Kaddish during the Period of Mourning and on the anniversary of a loved one's death. As we remember our departed, we perpetuate their presence among us. By remembering them we confer upon them the gift of immortality.

—Sidney Greenberg and Jonathan D. Levine

## A Personal Meditation

Eternal God, Master of mercy, give me the gift of remembering. May my memories of the dead be tender and true, neither diminished by time nor falsified by sentimentality. Let me recall them, and love them, as they were. Grant me the gift of tears. Let me express my sense of loss, my sorrow, my pain, as well as my gratitude and my love. Bless me with the gift of prayer. May I confront You with an open heart, with trusting faith, unembarrassed and unashamed. Strengthen me with the gift of hope. May I never lose faith in the beauty of life, the power of goodness, the right to joy. May I surrender my being, and the soul of the dead, to Your eternal compassion.

# A Yizkor Meditation in Memory of a Parent Who Was Hurtful

By Bob Saks

Dear God,
You know my heart.
Indeed,
You know me better than I know myself,
so I turn to You
before I rise for Kaddish.

My emotions swirl as I say this prayer.
The parent I remember was not kind to me.
His/Her death left me
with a legacy of unhealed wounds,
of anger
and of dismay
that a parent could hurt a child as I was hurt.
I do not want to pretend to love,
or to grieve what I do not feel,
but I do want to do what is right
as a Jew and as a child.

Help me, O God,
to subdue my bitter emotions
that do me no good,
and to find that place in myself
where happier memories may lie hidden,

and where grief for all that could have been,
all that should have been,
may be calmed by forgiveness,
or at least be soothed by the passage of time.

I pray that You,
who raises up slaves to freedom,
will liberate me from the oppression
of my hurt and anger,
and that You will lead me from this desert
to Your holy place,
Amen.

# Selective Bibliography

Brener, Anne. *Mourning and Mitzvah*. Woodstock: Jewish Lights, 1993.
———. *Taking The Time You Need to Mourn Your Loss*. (Life Lights). Woodstock: Jewish Lights, 2000.
De Sola Pool, David. *The Kaddish*. New York: Sivan Press, 1964.
Diamat, Anita. *Saying Kaddish*. New York: Schocken, 1998.
Gillman, Neil. *The Death of Death, Resurrection and Immortality in Jewish Thought*. Woodstock: Jewish Lights, 1997.
Goldberg, Chaim. *Mourning in Halahah*. New York: Mesorah, 1999.
Greenberg, Sidney (Editor). *A Treasury of Comfort*. Hollywood: Wilshire, 1967.
Hoffman, Lawrence A. *Canonization of the Synagogue Service*. London: University of Notre Dame Press, 1979.
Klein, Issac. *A Guide to Jewish Religious Practice*. New York: The Jewish Theological Seminary of America, 1992.
Kolatch, Alfred J. *The Jewish Mourners' Book of Why*. New York: Jonathan David, 1993.
Lamm, Maurice. *The Jewish Way in Death and Mourning*. New York: Jonathan David, 1994.
Levine, Aaron. *To Comfort the Bereaved: A Guide for Mourners and Those Who Visit Them*. New Jersey: Jason Aaronson, 1996.
Riemer, Jack (Editor). *Jewish Reflections on Death*. New York: Schocken, 1974.
Scherman, Nosson. *The Kaddish Prayer*. New York: Mesorah, 1997.
Solomon, Lewis D. *The Jewish Book of Living and Dying*. New Jersey: Jason Aaronson, 1999.
Spitz, Elie Kaplan. *Does the Soul Survive? A Jewish Journey to Belief in Afterlife, Past Lives and Living With Purpose*. Woodstock: Jewish Lights, 2000.
Steinsaltz, Adin. *Simple Words*. New York: Simon & Schuster, 1999.
Telsner, David. *The Kaddish: Its History and Significance*. Jerusalem: Tal Orot Institute, 1995.

Weiseltier, Leon. *Kaddish*. New York: Knopf, 1998.

Wolfson, Ron. *A Time to Mourn: A Time to Comfort*. New York: The Federation of Jewish Men's Clubs, 1993.

# Index

**Herbert A. Yoskowitz** is a Rabbi of the Adat Shalom Synagogue, Farmington Hills, Michigan. He holds a master of arts degree in clinical psychology from the University of Florida, as well as a master of Hebrew literature degree, Rabbinic ordination and honorary doctor of divinity degree from The Jewish Theological Seminary of America. The author of numerous articles and book reviews, Rabbi Yoskowitz has served on the editorial board of *Conservative Judaism* magazine. He has received specialized training in crisis and chemical dependency counseling, with special emphasis on bioethics, and has served in local, regional and national leadership positions with the Conservative Jewish Movement.

## What Others Say About *The Kaddish Minyan: The Impact on Ten Lives:*

"OUR PRAYER BOOKS now vary by denomination but the Kaddish speaks to and for all of us. And so does [this book] . . . Kaddish means "to sanctify." This book sanctifies and adds meaning to the central prayer and the central experience that we all share . . . "—**Rabbi Mitchell Wohlberg, Beth Tfiloh Congregation, Baltimore, Maryland**

". . . A POWERFUL AND POIGNANT SERIES of meditations on the Kaddish prayer, and the experience of mourning. Readers of all faiths will benefit from its deepening insights."—**Rabbi David Wolpe, Sinai Temple, Los Angeles, California; Author, *Making Loss Matter***

"WHAT A BEAUTIFUL, POWERFUL BOOK! *The Kaddish Minyan* has opened this Christian's eyes to the profound spiritual experience of saying Kaddish with others...should be read by Christians as well as Jews . . . "
—**Reverend David Blewett, Executive Director, The Ecumenical Institute for Jewish-Christian Studies, Southfield, Michigan**

"RABBI YOSKOWITZ HAS GATHERED . . . a rich collection of personal reflections by people for whom bereavement became a path to spiritual renewal. These messages can do the same for many of us as we struggle to make sense out of life just when it seems hardest to do so."—**Rabbi Mark G. Loeb, Beth El Congregation, Baltimore, Maryland**

"RABBI YOSKOWITZ'S BOOK IS A GIFT . . . While the experience of mourning is universal, and the words of Kaddish are fixed, this book allows us to hear a myriad of distinct voices that inspire us to seek our own reservoirs of comfort from the wellsprings of the Kaddish tradition."
—**Rabbi E.B. Freedman, Director, Jewish Hospice and Chaplaincy Network, Southfield, Michigan**